Let's Play:
MURDER.

Matt Longstaff and Chris Walker

Aa

is for
Asphyxiation

Bb

is for
Beheading

Cc

is for
Crushed

Dd

is for

Drowning

Ee

is for

Electrocution

Ff

is for

Freezing

Gg

is for
Gas

Hh

is for

Hanging

Ii

is for

Incineration

Jj

is for
Jousting

Kk

is for
Knuckle sandwich

Ll

is for

Lobotomy

Mm

is for
Missed

Nn

is for
Neglect

Oo

is for
Overdose

Pp

is for
Plunge

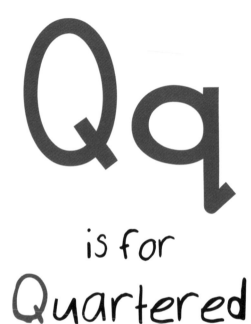

is for
Quartered

Rr

is for
Rabies

Ss

is for
Skewered

Tt

is for
Trauma

Uu

is for

Unplugged

Vv

is for

Voodoo

Ww

is for

Woodchipper

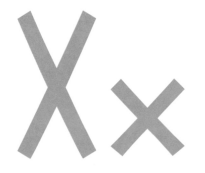

is for
Xylophone

Yy

is for

Yoga

Zz

is for
Zombies

Learn how to draw

1   2   3   4

the Sinister Siblings

1   2   3   4

THIS IS A DEAD CANARY BOOK

Copyright © 2015 by Matt Longstaff, Chris Walker & Dead Canary Books

Published in Great Britain in 2015 by Dead Canary Books

Dead Canary Books
13 Holywell Row
London
EC2A 4JF

deadcanarybooks.com

Cover design by Chris Walker
Typeface design by Momo Tanaka-Betts

A CIP catalogue for this book is available from the British Library

ISBN 978-0-99287-318-9

Printed in the UK by Steve Hannah

Special thanks to K. Jenkins and C.F. Peel

www.letsplaymurder.com